16.99 LG

P9-DNQ-110

Ron's BIG MISSION

Rose Blue and Corinne J. Naden

illustrated by Don Tate

· Dutton ·
Children's
Books

To Autumn (Shawn) and Jheris: I believe in you, baby girls.
Accomplish your missions. —D.T.

Thanks to: Lake City Library, a branch of the Florence County Library System; Lance
B. Linton, a photographer who went over and beyond the call of duty to get access
to the original library to provide me with visual reference.

—D.T.

DUTTON CHILDREN'S BOOKS • A division of Penguin Young Readers Group

Published by the Penguin Group

Penguin Group (USA) Inc., 375 Hudson Street, New York, New York 10014, U.S.A. • Penguin Group (Canada), 90 Eglington Avenue East, Toronto, Ontario M4P 2Y3,
Canada (a division of Pearson Penguin Canada Inc.) • Penguin Books Ltd, 80 Strand, London WC2R 0RL, England • Penguin Ireland, 25 St Stephen's Green, Dublin
2, Ireland (a division of Penguin Books Ltd) • Penguin Group (Australia), 250 Camberwell Road, Camberwell, Victoria 3124, Australia (a division of Pearson Australia
Group Pty Ltd) • Penguin Books India Pvt Ltd, 11 Community Centre, Panchsheel Park, New Delhi—110 017, India • Penguin Group (NZ), 67 Apollo Drive, Rosedale,
North Shore 0632, New Zealand (a division of Pearson New Zealand Ltd) • Penguin Books (South Africa) (Pty) Ltd, 24 Sturdee Avenue, Rosebank, Johannesburg
2196, South Africa • Penguin Books Ltd, Registered Offices: 80 Strand, London WC2R 0RL, England

Library of Congress Cataloging-in-Publication Data
Blue, Rose.
Ron on a mission / by Rose Blue and Corinne J. Naden ; illustrated by Don Tate.—1st ed.
p. cm.
Summary: One summer day in 1959, nine-year-old Ron McNair, who dreams of being a pilot one day, walks into the Lake City,
South Carolina, public library and insists on checking out some books, despite the rule that only white people can have library
cards. Includes facts about McNair, who grew up to be an astronaut.
ISBN: 978-0-525-47849-2
1. McNair, Ronald E., 1950–1986—Childhood and youth—Juvenile fiction. [1. McNair, Ronald E., 1950–1986—Child-
hood and youth—Fiction. 2. Segregation—Fiction. 3. Libraries—Fiction. 4. Books and reading—Fiction.
5. African Americans—Fiction. 6. South Carolina—History—20th century—
Fiction.] I. Naden, Corinne J.
II. Tate, Don, ill. III. Title.
PZ7.B6248Ron 2008
[E]—dc22   2007050563

Published in the United States by Dutton Children's Books,
a division of Penguin Young Readers Group
345 Hudson Street, New York, New York 10014
www.penguin.com/youngreaders

Designed by Jason Henry
Manufactured in China
First Edition
1 3 5 7 9 10 8 6 4 2

"You're up early this morning, Ron. What's the rush?" asked Mrs. McNair. "Come and have your breakfast. I made some oatmeal."

"I have to go, Momma," said Ron, tying his sneakers. "I have something to do this morning."

"You *always* have something to do," said his mother with a smile. "Just be home by lunchtime, okay?"

Ron was nine years old. That morning he left his house with a plan. He'd been thinking about it for a long time. It was a beautiful South Carolina summer day, and Ron looked up at the blue, blue sky.

Someday, he thought, he would be up there, flying a plane. He wanted to be a pilot when he grew up. But today Ron had something else on his mind—something very important.

Ron walked down the street as fast as he could. He didn't want to be late.

"Hi, Ron," the grocer called from the front of his store. "There you are. Just in time for a doughnut."

"Morning, Mr. Douglas," said Ron. "Thank you, but there's someplace I've got to be." And Ron kept on walking.

FRESH
BAKED BREAD

ICE C

RICE
CEREAL

RICE
CEREAL

JUICY
APPLES

own by the schoolyard Ron saw his friend Carl shooting baskets.
"All right! You made it!" called Carl.

"Hi, Carl," said Ron. "I wish I could stay, but I've got something important to do."

"More important than basketball on summer vacation?" said Carl. "Are you kidding?"

Ron laughed. He loved to play basketball but not today. Today was too important. Ron kept on walking.

When Ron got to the Lake City Public Library, he stopped. This was it. He was hot from walking so fast, and he was nervous, too. He took a deep breath, lifted his head high, and went inside.

Mrs. Scott was busy getting ready for all the people who would be using the library today. As the head librarian she had to make sure that everything was neat and orderly. Mrs. Scott looked up to welcome her first visitor of the day. She smiled as Ron walked in. He was her best customer. Ron gave a little wave to Mrs. Scott and went right to the shelves.

t took Ron a while to find some books. He always looked for books that showed children who looked like him. But that was hard. There were not many books about black kids on the shelves.

At last Ron found some books on airplanes. He took the books and started to walk to the front desk. Ron felt nervous and his hands felt a little sweaty, but he knew what he wanted to do. Mrs. Fielding, a white lady who was often in the library, stopped him. "You can give me the books and I'll check them out for you, Ron," she said gently.

"No, thanks, Mrs. Fielding," Ron said. "I'm going to do it all by myself."

"But, Ron—" she started to say.

Ron was already on his way to the front desk. He put the books on the counter.

"I'd like to check these out, please," said Ron.

The desk clerk didn't look at him. *Didn't she hear me?* Ron wondered.

Ron knew what he had to do.

He jumped up on the counter. He wanted the desk clerk to know he was serious.

"I'd like to check out these books," he said quietly.

At first the desk clerk and Mrs. Scott just looked at each other. "You know you can't check out books, Ron," said Mrs. Scott. "You can read them here. That's the rule. Only white people can check out books from the library."

Ron looked at Mrs. Scott and the desk clerk politely. But he would not budge.

"I always read them here. Today, I want to check them out," said Ron.

Mrs. Scott and the desk clerk did not know what to do. Ron wouldn't get off the counter. People were staring. Finally, the desk clerk called the Lake City police.

Two policemen came right over.

"Let someone check out the books for you, son," said one of the policemen. "You know the rules."

But Ron just shook his head—he would not budge.

Now, Mrs. Scott called Ron's mother. Mrs. McNair came to the library very quickly. "I know how you feel, baby," she said. "But you have to follow the rules."

"I can't, Momma," Ron told her. "It's wrong. The rules are not fair. Why can't I check out books like everyone else?"

No one said anything—not the desk clerk, not Mrs. Scott, not the policemen. Not even Ron's mother.

Mrs. Scott looked at Ron. She thought about all the times that Ron came into the library and all the times he sat at the tables for hours looking over so many books. He was her best customer—and *she* knew what she had to do.

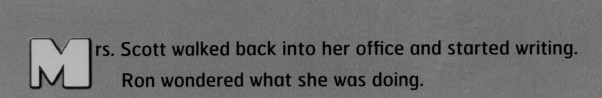

Mrs. Scott walked back into her office and started writing.
Ron wondered what she was doing.

Mrs. Scott returned and handed Ron a library card. *His* library card.

Ron looked at Mrs. Scott and smiled. As he jumped to the floor, he thought he saw her smile, too.

"I'd like to check out these books, please," he said handing the card to the desk clerk.

The desk clerk took his library card and stamped the cards in the back of the books. "These are due back in two weeks," she said.

on smiled. "Thank you," he said. He tucked the books under his arm and took his mother's hand. Together, they walked home. Ron couldn't wait to get to his room…

...and open to page one.

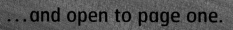

AUTHOR'S NOTE

The boy who was Ron McNair grew into a man who flew planes just like he dreamed he would do. He became an astronaut. Today, everyone in Lake City remembers him. They remember him every time they walk into the library. The red brick building on 234 Main Street is a special place. The walls in the children's room were painted with pictures that show children reading books under a huge oak tree. A space shuttle flies through the sky.

Inside the library, anyone can get a card and check out books. Young Ron McNair had a dream. On that day in 1959, he made it start to come true. Because of him, many young people have a chance to dream.

"You can only be a winner if you are willing to walk over the edge," astronaut McNair once told a group of children. "You're eagles. Spread your wings and fly to the sky."

Many years ago in Lake City, South Carolina, young Ron McNair became a hero. Years later, in 1986, astronaut Ron McNair was once again a hero. He lost his life when the space shuttle *Challenger* exploded on January 28, with the loss of the entire crew. The Lake City Public Library is dedicated to astronaut McNair.

This story is a fictionalized account of a real incident in Ron McNair's life. There are several versions of this story. This version comes from interviews with Ron's mother, the late Mrs. McNair, and Gloria Wilson, administrative assistant to the director of library systems in Florence County, South Carolina; and Gloria Tisdale of the Lake City School District. We thank them for their help in reconstructing this inspirational story. Except for Mrs. McNair and Ron, all of the character names are fictional.